MW01629354

Animals

LIVE. LEARN. DISCOVER.

Bath · New York · Singapore · Hong Kong · Cologne · Delhi · Melbourne

First published by Parragon in 2009

Parragon
Queen Street House
4 Queen Street
Bath BA1 1HE, UK

ISBN 978-1-4075-8086-9

Printed in China

Contents

On the wing

Birds have wings instead of arms. They fly by extending and flapping their wings. The wings are made from a number of bones with feathers attached to them. Wings can be long and broad, or short and narrow.

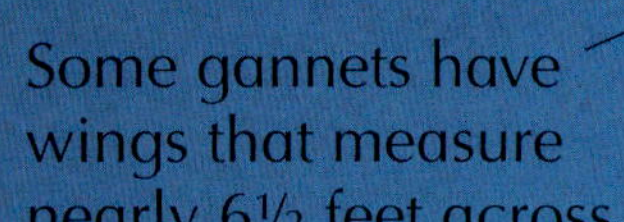

Some gannets have wings that measure nearly 6½ feet across.

Gliding through air

Gliding birds, such as gannets, use currents of moving air to fly. These birds have very large wings that catch the currents and carry the birds into the air.

Wing shapes

Birds that fly by gliding and soaring, such as eagles and gulls, have large wings with long feathers. Birds that fly short distances and need to dart about quickly, such as robins, pheasants, and swallows, have short wings that they flap quickly.

Fast flight

Swallows have short wings that let
them fly quickly and dart about to
catch flying insects. If they need to
dive, they pull their wings into their
bodies and drop like a stone.

Some hummingbirds
flap their wings 1,200
times a minute.

Hovering hummingbirds

Hummingbirds are small birds
that can hover. They stay in one
place by beating their wings
backward and forward very
quickly. This lets them hover in
front of a flower, so that they can
reach in and drink nectar.

Flying insects

Most insects have two pairs of wings, which they use to fly. Insect wings vary in shape, from the tiny wings of bees to the large, colorful wings of butterflies.

Hard to catch

Houseflies have only one pair of wings, but they are still among the fastest insects. They use their speed to escape attackers.

Insect hunters

Dragonflies have two pairs of long, see-through wings. These powerful insects are excellent fliers, and can catch smaller insects in midair.

Dragonflies have large eyes for finding prey.

Buzzing bees

The honeybee has two
pairs of very thin wings.
It beats these wings
so quickly that they
make a buzzing
sound. A bee can fly
at 20 miles per hour.

Did you know?

Most insects do not use
their mouths to make sounds.
Instead, they rub their wings
or legs together to make
a noise.

Colorful butterflies

Butterfly wings are covered in tiny
scales. These scales can be a wide
variety of colors.

Ladybug wings

The ladybug has a pair of
tough, spotted outer wings.
These cover a second pair of
wings, which are very delicate.
The ladybug uses the second
pair for flying.

Life in the rain forest

Most rain-forest animals live high in the trees. This is called the canopy. They have learned how to move from tree to tree and where to find food and water. Some animals never come down to the ground.

Orange ape

Orangutans have long arms and legs. Their fingers are hooked to help them grip branches as they climb through the trees looking for fruit.

Did you know?

Although most chameleons eat insects, a few species are big enough to catch and eat birds.

Colorful beak

The toucan eats fruit. It uses its long beak to reach fruit that grows at the ends of small branches.

Insects in the canopy

Many different kinds of insects are found in the canopy, where they eat leaves. These insects may be eaten by larger animals, such as birds or lizards.

Tough beak

The scarlet macaw has a powerful hooked beak. It uses this to crack open nuts and as an extra claw to climb up the trunks of trees.

Clever camouflage

Chameleons can change the color of their skin so that they blend in with the leaves of the trees. This is called camouflage and it makes chameleons difficult to see.

Mixed forests

Temperate forests are found in cool parts of the world. They are a mixture of trees that lose their leaves in winter (deciduous trees) and trees that keep their leaves during the cold months (evergreen trees).

Losing leaves

Deciduous trees lose their leaves because they do not get enough water in the winter. The water in the ground freezes, making it impossible for trees to collect it through their roots. The leaves turn brown and fall off.

Millipedes eat the leaves that fall off the trees.

Living on the floor

The forest floor is covered in plants and fallen leaves. These make it an ideal home for many small animals, such as millipedes.

Forest birds

Temperate forests are home to many birds. The birds eat the seeds and fruit that grow on the trees, as well as insects living there. The birds also build nests in the branches.

Wrens hunt for insects in holes and cracks on trees.

Wild boar

Wild boar are large pigs that live in forests. They eat roots, fruit, and berries that lie on the forest floor. Male boars have curved teeth called tusks, which stick out of their mouths.

Did you know?

The largest tree, the Sequoia, can grow to more than 330 feet tall and live for 2,000 years.

Warm grasslands

Grasslands are large areas of flat ground covered by grasses. Warm grasslands, or savannahs, are found in Africa, South America, and Australia. During the dry months the grasses turn yellow. However, once the rains fall, the grasslands turn green.

The hyena is often called the laughing hyena because of its noisy cackle or laughlike call.

A sea of grass

Some of the grasses on the savannah are taller than people. There are only a few trees, such as acacias and baobabs. Most of the young trees are eaten before they can grow very tall.

Bone-crushing hyenas

Spotted hyenas are hunters that live on the grasslands of Africa. They have strong jaws and huge teeth that can crush the bones of their prey as if they were twigs.

30 cute animal stickers to decorate your stuff!

The great migration

Each year, huge herds of zebras and wildebeest make long journeys in search of fresh grass to eat. This is called a migration. The migration is dangerous because the animals have to cope with fast-flowing rivers and hunters, such as crocodiles.

Meerkats keep a sharp eye out for hunters, such as snakes or jackals.

On guard

Meerkats live in large groups in burrows under the grasslands of southern Africa. Each member of the group has a job to do. Some are babysitters or teachers, while others are guards or hunters.

Cool grasslands

Grasslands found in the cooler parts of the world are called temperate grasslands. These regions are warm in the summer and may be covered in snow in the winter.

Digging hunter

The badger uses its long, sharp claws to dig small animals, such as ground squirrels and mice, out of the ground.

Rabbits thump the ground with their back legs to warn other rabbits of danger.

Good listener

The rabbit has long ears, which give it a good sense of hearing. It uses these to listen for any hunters that may be nearby.

Red fox

The red fox is a carnivore, or meat eater. It is usually active at night, when it hunts for small mammals, such as rabbits. It also feeds on berries.

Did you know?

A single pair of rabbits will have as many as 40 babies in a year.

Pack animals

Llamas are found on the grassy slopes of the Andes Mountains in South America. These plant eaters live in groups called herds and are used by local people to carry heavy loads.

Llamas are related to camels.

Lakes and ponds

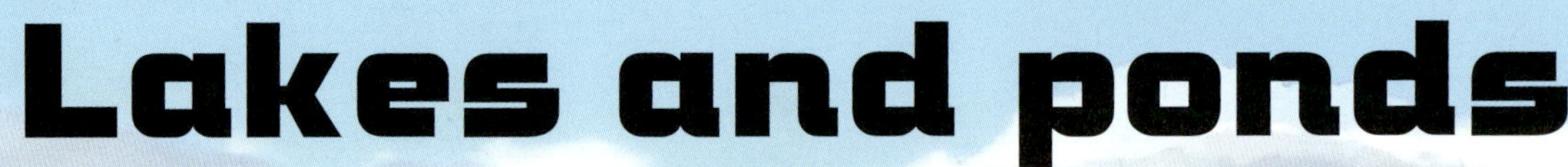

The water in ponds and lakes is called still water because it hardly moves. Animals living there do not have to swim against a flow of water, as they do in streams and rivers.

Plant life

Plants, such as reeds, grow in the shallow water around the edges of lakes and ponds. Many animals like to hide among the plant stems and eat the leaves.

This newt is brightly colored to warn other animals that it is poisonous.

Newts

Newts belong to a group of animals called amphibians. They spend most of their time swimming in the water, but they also have legs so that they can walk across land.

Freshwater fish

Many different kinds of fish are found in ponds and lakes, including this cichlid. Some fish feed on plants, while others hunt and eat other animals.

Plankton

Microscopic life

Pond water is full of tiny living things that are too small for us to see. These are called plankton and they include small plants, larvae (baby insects), and fish eggs.

Dragonfly larvae spend the first year of their lives in the water, hunting other animals.

Dragonfly larvae

Dragonflies lay their eggs in water. The young that hatch from the eggs are called larvae. When the larvae become adults, they leave the water and fly away.

The Arctic

The Arctic is the region around the North Pole. This icy world has very long winters. In the middle of winter, the sun sets and does not rise again for several weeks.

Changing ice sheet

The Arctic is covered by a thick sheet of ice. During the summer, some of the ice melts and the sheet gets smaller. This means that land hunters, such as polar bears, have less area to hunt in, and they can struggle to find food.

Keeping warm

Seals have a thick layer of fat, called blubber, just beneath their skin. This keeps the seals warm in the icy Arctic seas.

Multi-colored beaks

Puffins catch small fish to eat and to feed to their young. They hold the fish in their colorful beaks and carry about ten fish at a time.

Did you know?

Puffins are very good swimmers and can dive to depths of 200 feet to look for fish.

A new coat

The Arctic fox changes the color of its coat during the year to blend in with its surroundings. In winter, it has a white coat to hide in the snow. In summer, it turns brown to match the rocks and soil.

Locust swarms

Locusts form groups called swarms. They fly out of the desert and eat whole crops in neighboring regions.

Hot deserts

Most deserts are hot during the day, so animals creep under bushes or into holes to escape the sun. At night, the temperatures fall and it can be very cold.

The fox's large ears are very good at hearing prey running across the sand.

Nighttime hunter

Bat-eared foxes avoid the heat of the desert by sleeping in burrows during the day. They come out at night to hunt when it is cooler.

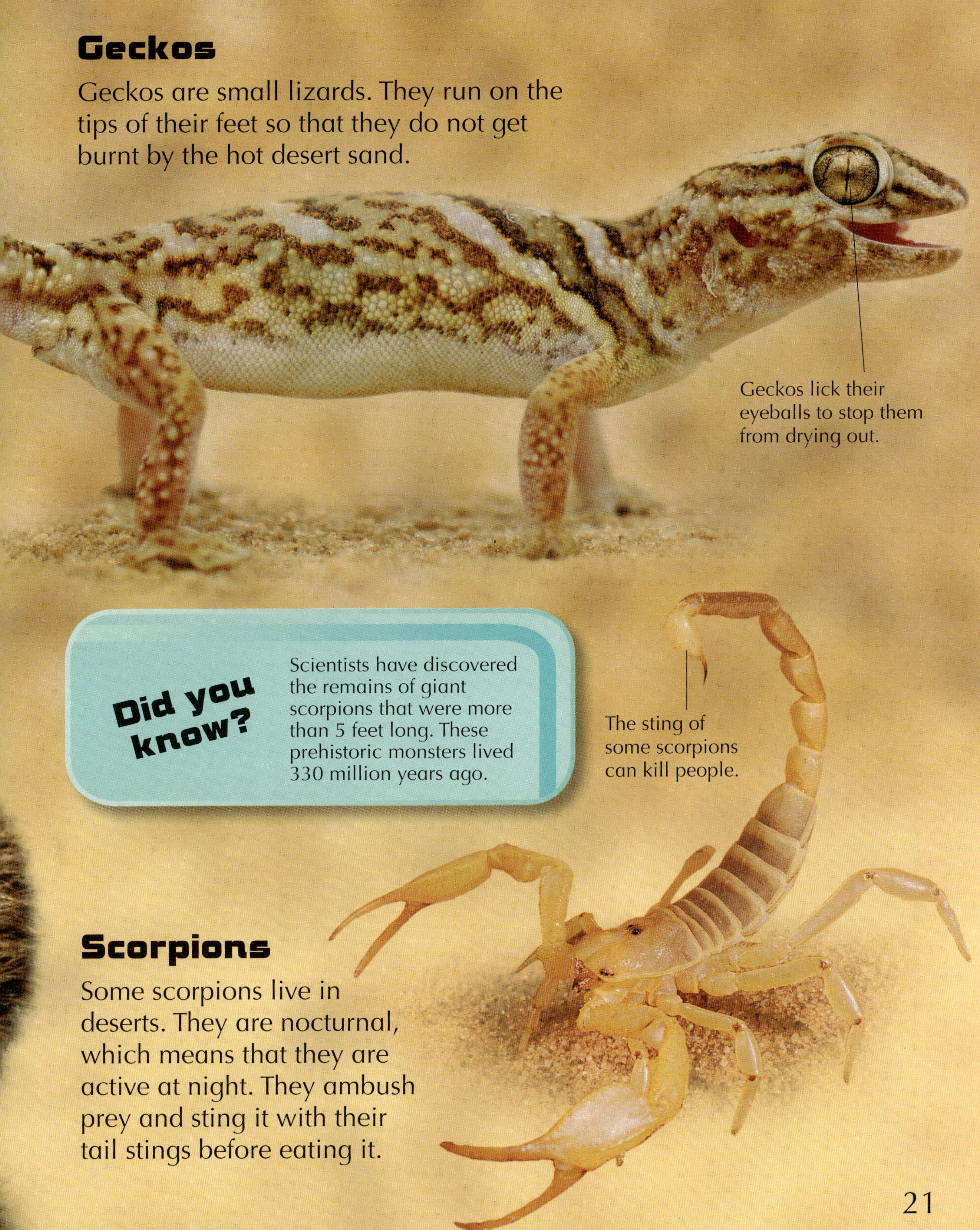

Geckos

Geckos are small lizards. They run on the tips of their feet so that they do not get burnt by the hot desert sand.

Geckos lick their eyeballs to stop them from drying out.

Scientists have discovered the remains of giant scorpions that were more than 5 feet long. These prehistoric monsters lived 330 million years ago.

The sting of some scorpions can kill people.

Scorpions

Some scorpions live in deserts. They are nocturnal, which means that they are active at night. They ambush prey and sting it with their tail stings before eating it.

Extinct is forever

Animals become extinct (die out) for many reasons, such as a change in their habitat. For example, if the climate gets warmer, the animal may not survive this change.

Ancient animals

Crocodiles are ancient animals that were around when dinosaurs roamed the earth. Unlike the dinosaurs, crocodiles have survived. Other ancient animals still around include alligators and tortoises.

Terrible lizards

Dinosaurs disappeared 65 million years ago. They became extinct because the world's climate changed. The dinosaurs could not survive this change, so they died out.

Dinosaurs, such as *Tyrannosaurus Rex*, could not survive in the new climate.

Did you know?

In 2006, the World Conservation Union published a list of 16,119 animals, plants, and fungi that are at risk of become extinct.

Hunted to death

Dodos were a kind of flightless bird that lived on Mauritius in the Indian Ocean. They became extinct in the 1600s because they were hunted by humans.

Under threat

Many well-known animals could become extinct in the next 10 years or so, including the giant panda, tiger, and black rhino. A few of these animals survive in national parks and zoos, where they are protected.

Acknowledgments

All artwork supplied by Myke Taylor, The Art Agency.

Photo credits:
b—bottom, t—top, r—right, l—left, m—middle

Cover: Front—Daniel J. Cox/GettyImages, back—Gail Shumway/GettyImages.

Poster: Dreamstime.com/Anthony Hathaway.

Internals:
1 Dreamstime.com/David Davis, 2tl Dreamstime.com/Kiyoshi Takahase Segundo, 2tr Dreamstime.com/Fred Goldstein, 2ml Dreamstime.com/Carolyne Pehora, 2–3m Digital Vision, 3b Dreamstime.com/Wei Send Chen, 4 Digital Vision, 5tr Dreamstime.com/Willie Manalo, 5tl Digital Vision, 5br Dreamstime.com/Kiyoshi Takahase Segundo, 6tr Digital Vision, 6b Dreamstime.com/Bobby Deal, 7tr Dreamstime.com/Fred Goldstein, 7br Dreamstime.com/Sanja Stepanovic, 8tl Dreamstime.com/Phil Date, 8br Dreamstime.com/Kathy Wynn, 9tr Dreamstime.com, 9m Tall Tree Ltd, 9b Dreamstime.com/Michael Ledray, 10tl Digital Vision, 10bl Digital Vision, 11t Dreamstime.com/Robert Hambley, 11b Dreamstime.com/Jorge Felix Costa, 12–13 Dreamstime.com/Stefan Ekernas, 12bl Dreamstime.com, 13m Digital Vision, 13r Dreamstime.com, 14t Digital Vision, 14b Dreamstime.com/Joe Gough, 15t Dreamstime.com, 15b Dreamstime.com/Andreas Steinbach, 16t Dreamstime.com/Mike Brake, 16b Dreamstime.com/Michael L., 17t Dreamstime.com/Dallas Powell, Jr., 17b Dreamstime.com/Holger Leyrer, 18t Dreamstime.com/Anthony Hathaway, 18b Dreamstime.com/Steffen Foerster, 19t Dreamstime.com, 19b Dreamstime.com/Holger Wulschlaeger, 20tl Dreamstime.com/Steve Schowiak, 20b Dreamstime.com/Vladimir Pomortsev, 21t Dreamstime.com, 21b Digital Vision, 22 Dreamstime.com/Fah mun Kwan, 23br Dreamstime.com/Nico Smit.